THE EASY WAY TO BECOME WEALTHY

DISCOVER THE SECRETS OF MAKING MONEY AND ACHIEVING FINANCIAL FREEDOM

JOHN A. KASPER

ISBN: 9798872015772

First Edition: 2023

Contents

PART 1: FOUNDATIONS OF WEALTH
Chapter 1: Introduction: Unveiling the Secrets to Financial Freedom
Chapter 2: Defining Your Wealth: What Does Financial Freedom Mean to You?
Chapter 3: Building a Strong Financial Foundation: Budgeting, Debt Management, and Savings
Chapter 4: Developing a Wealth Mindset: Shifting Your Perspective on Money and Abundance

PART 2: STRATEGIES FOR WEALTH CREATION
Chapter 5: Investing for Growth: Exploring Different Investment Vehicles and Strategies

Chapter 6: Generating Passive Income: Creating Multiple Streams of Revenue

Chapter 7: Building Your Career: Strategies for Earning More and Achieving Financial Goals

Chapter 8: Entrepreneurship: Launching Your Business and Achieving Financial Independence

PART 3: MAINTAINING AND GROWING YOUR WEALTH

Chapter 9: Protecting Your Assets: Insurance, Risk Management, and Estate Planning

Chapter 10: Leaving a Legacy: Philanthropy, Financial Literacy, and Empowering Others

<u>**CONCLUSION**</u>

PART 1: FOUNDATIONS OF WEALTH

Chapter 1: Introduction: Unveiling the Secrets to Financial Freedom

Are you fed up with barely making ends meet? Do you want to live a life devoid of anxiety and stress related to money? You're not alone yourself. Many people struggle in today's environment to attain security and financial independence.

However, there's no need to worry—in this chapter of the book, I'll reveal the key to real financial independence. You'll be well on your way to a life of prosperity and financial security with these strategies and techniques.

What is Financial Freedom?

Financial independence or financial freedom is simply living comfortably and stress-free. This is a word that has gained popularity in recent years. It entails having sufficient income to meet your needs and the flexibility to follow your interests and ambitions unhindered by financial obligations.

However, what does achieving financial independence entail? I'll go into more detail about financial independence in this chapter of the book and show you how to discover its mysteries.

Having financial control is the fundamental component of financial independence. It's more important to be able to make decisions that are consistent with your ideals and aspirations without having to worry about money than it is to be wealthy or debt-free. This might include going for a profession you're enthusiastic about as opposed to one that pays well but brings you no joy. It could also imply having the resources to take early retirement or tour the globe.

It's important to first define financial independence for yourself to fully comprehend what it entails. Depending on their unique objectives and interests, each person may have a distinct notion of financial independence. While some may define it as being able to live off of passive income sources, others may define it as having a certain amount of funds in their bank account.

The four pillars of financial independence are debt management, investing, saving, and budgeting.

Creating Reasonable Goals to Reach Financial Independence

We'll talk about how important it is to have reasonable objectives to reach financial independence in this part.

With materialism at its height in today's fast-paced society, it's simple to fall into the trap of living above our means and overpaying. Many individuals thus discover that they are always battling debt and unstable finances. However, reaching financial independence is not insurmountable if you have the correct attitude and strategy.

Setting attainable objectives is the first step towards financial independence. Knowing exactly where you are financially now and where you want to go in the future is crucial. This will assist you in planning your route to financial independence.

It's critical to establish objectives that are both quantifiable and precise. For example, establish a monthly or annual savings goal rather than just declaring, "*I want to save more money.*" This will enable you to monitor your progress in addition to providing you to strive towards.

Being honest with oneself is another essential component of creating objectives that are doable for reaching financial independence. We often have a tendency to overestimate our income and underestimate our costs, which makes it harder to reach our unreasonable ambitions.

Practical Tips for Managing Your Finances Properly

Although handling our money could sometimes seem like a difficult undertaking, it is crucial to reaching financial independence. Having enough money to support oneself gives us a feeling of security and peace of mind and enables us to live the lives we want. However, prudent money management is now more important than ever due to the rising cost of living and the persistent desire to spend more than we can afford.

I will provide some useful advice in this area that will enable you to manage your money and eventually discover the key to financial independence. Financial professionals have tried and tested these suggestions, and they work well in assisting people in reaching their financial goals.

- **Make a budget**: Setting up a budget is the first step to prudent financial management. This can help you manage your money wisely by providing you with a clear picture of your income and spending. Make sure your budget accounts for all required costs, including bills, food, rent or mortgage payments, and savings.

- **Keep track of your spending**: If we don't keep track of our costs, it's simple to overspend without realising it. Track your spending patterns using tools like online spreadsheets and budgeting applications. This will assist you in identifying potential areas of expenditure and implementing the required changes.

- **Make conserving money your top priority**: Greetings and welcome to our part in finding the key to financial independence! The significance of investing and saving for long-term financial security will be covered in this section. A lot of individuals want to be financially independent, but not many realise how important saving and investing are to bringing that goal to pass.

Let me first clarify what I mean about financial independence. It is the capacity to live comfortably without being dependent on one's income or worrying about money. If your primary source of income were to abruptly disappear, you would still be able to support your preferred lifestyle and pay for your bills provided you had sufficient savings and investments.

Why then are investing and saving so important for long-term financial security? The short explanation is that it facilitates the gradual accumulation of wealth. You are practically building a safety net for yourself in case of any unanticipated events by setting aside a percentage of your salary and investing it. Knowing that you have a financial safety net to fall back on will give you peace of mind.

Moreover, investing and saving enables you to expand your money. Even while it would seem secure to just put your money in a savings account, investment yields a higher rate of return. You may invest your money in a variety of assets, including stocks, bonds, and real estate.

The Six Easy Steps to Financial Independence

It turns out that the key to financial independence is not as ostentatious as you may have previously believed. In actuality, making thoughtful financial decisions and cautious preparation now will pay off in the long run. These are the things that we believe are most important:

1. Avoid giving in to the inflation of luxury and live within your means.

A typical mistake made by those who want to save and accumulate money is to equate a rise in wages with increased spending. For instance, receiving a pay increase does not always indicate that purchasing the Tesla you've always wanted—even if it is just barely within your means—is a wise financial move. The prudent manage their finances by setting aside extra money for investments, whether they are savings or investments in the future.

2. Invest your money to take advantage of the difficult inflation.

Inflation, expressed simply, is the loss of the prior worth of money. This implies that money in a savings account loses value just because it is kept there, even if it is not being used. Investing your money and taking advantage of compound interest is the greatest approach to combat inflation.

3. Budgeting may help you remain focused and disciplined.

Making a budget helps you plan where your money is going and how you will use it, which is the best method to stay on track. Budgeting is a tool used by the most frugal people to pay for basics, save what they need, and invest surplus money. You have more control and suffer less financial worry the more you budget.

4. Have an emergency fund for three months.

Emergencies are unanticipated and can pose a serious risk to individuals. By creating an emergency fund, you provide yourself with a safety net to prevent unforeseen circumstances from impeding your financial success. You have, as it were, included the emergency in your spending plan.

5. Make self-care a priority.

If we are not well, we are nothing. The working hard lifestyle is highly promoted in today's society, however, it often fails to encourage individuals to take breaks and recharge. When you put self-care first, you make sure that you can keep working towards your objectives without having to worry about burnout or diseases brought on by stress and overwork.

6. Invest time in your financial education.

To put it simply, you may develop more the more you know. It's critical to understand that you should set aside some money to enable you to get further knowledge about how it functions. Books, podcasts, courses, and other mediums may be used for this. You may utilise your understanding of money to your advantage and make the best choices for yourself.

Chapter 2: Defining Your Wealth: What Does Financial Freedom Mean to You?

There are a lot of ways to feel free when it comes to your financial health. We go into the idea of financial independence and show you how to define and ultimately attain it for yourself.

Financial Freedom: What Is It?

Many of us have aspirations of financial independence. However, what does it mean? Financial independence, in my opinion, looks different for everyone, despite what the financial industry may try to convince you of.

Moreover, your short- and long-term objectives, attitude, lifestyle, and culture may all influence the route you follow to financial independence. Here, we'll explore many perspectives on financial independence, obstacles you may encounter, and possible actions you may take to realise your dream of financial freedom. Now let's move!

What Is Inherent in Financial Freedom?

Excellent question. The response? Depending on the person you ask. To be financially free, according to some, is to have enough riches that you never have to worry about money again.

However, what freedom means to one person may not mean to another. Numerous variables come into play, such as your age, location, lifestyle, and aspirations.

Here are some guidelines to help you begin thinking about what financial independence means to you:

- Being financially independent and feeling in control of your money
- Staying on course to achieve your financial objectives
- Having sufficient funds on hand in case anything goes wrong
- having sufficient money to live a certain way
- All of them together result in a generalised feeling of financial security and confidence, or the ability to accomplish your goals stress-free.

To be able to effortlessly manage your finances and life in the manner that best suits you is our concept of financial freedom in its widest sense.

What Gives You a Sense of Financial Freedom?

Can you purchase freedom with money? Not quite, but it could provide you with the means to feel happier and more at ease. To be financially free for some of us is to be able to afford a boat voyage across the Caribbean. For others, it's having enough money to accomplish the things we like, or it's being able to buy creature pleasures.

While some of us are content to explore the world, others want to own a house. While some people would rather spend their money to live in the moment, others would rather work hard and save a lot of money to be able to afford retirement early. Ultimately, it comes down to having the freedom to make decisions that are ourselves without worrying about the financial consequences.

Here are some points to think about to provide you with a framework for defining financial independence according to your standards:

The Right to Free Will

Being financially or otherwise free means having the capacity to live the life you desire and making the decisions that are best for you. This might include earning so much money that you can allocate your time whatever you like. However, there are other ways to exercise your freedom of choice. One method is to advance in your industry and eventually be able to choose from a variety of well-paying positions. Alternatively, it may include working for an NGO, teaching overseas, or following a vocation as an artist. You may decide to work as a freelancer on inspiring initiatives or choose a profession that enables you to establish a family. Being financially free means that you can make decisions, which is a powerful feeling. It also implies that you may base your money management technique on your values and make choices that are relevant to you.

The Security Freedom

While some people prefer spontaneity over consistency, most people want security in one form or another. Financially speaking, security might be defined as long-term financial stability and dependability in revenue. It can also indicate that you have enough cash on hand to deal with unforeseen expenses or to comfortably look after your kids and other dependent family members. Some individuals define security as going above and beyond things like owning a house, making significant contributions to retirement funds, or having passive income streams like real estate or investments. It's important to consider what makes you feel safe, regardless of who you are, and to make the necessary financial adjustments to reach that goal.

The Adventurer's Freedom

Want the excitement of something fresh? For a lot of us, feeling free is mostly dependent on discovery and adventure. Including adventure in your life might lead to happiness, whether you choose to travel for business or pleasure, launch a thrilling new job, or take time off to travel or follow your hobbies. It's beneficial to consider how having financial independence might provide you with a feeling of adventure, whatever that may mean for you. You may choose a profession that enables you to travel the globe for a job or pleasure. Alternatively, you may save up a significant amount of money every month for a long trip, sabbatical, or early retirement, and then take off to see the globe.

The Comfort Zone's Freedom

What gives you a sense of ease and comfort? To be comfortable, for some individuals, is to have enough money to buy things that bring them joy and cosiness; for others, it means to have enough money in retirement accounts or the bank to be content with their quality of life. Which would you prefer—a comfy couch in a rural house or the balcony of a flat in the city? Are you more at ease with the idea of owning a house, or do you like the freedom of renting? At any stage of life, it's a good idea to define comfort and consider how it relates to your financial objectives.

The Ability to Choose

When considering financial independence, we believe that having the flexibility to spend your time as you please—at work, with your family, travelling, and everywhere in between! A lot of this depends on how you save and spend your money. Suppose your ideal retirement age is in your 40s or 50s. Perhaps you put in a lot of effort in the early years of your profession to reap the benefits of having free time in the future. Perhaps you've decided to work remotely so that you can spend more of your time travelling, or you've chosen a day job or part-time employment that allows you to devote more time to your hobbies.

In the end, achieving financial independence is striking a balance between your needs and goals and the money you have or expect to have in the future. The next step is to create objectives to reach the level of financial independence that you value, whether it is more time, security, or adventure. The favourable tidings? There are several ways to envision a happy life, not just one perfect or bad one!

What obstacles exist for financial independence?

In an ideal society, everyone would have access to enough money to maintain their health and happiness while avoiding debt. However, as we are all too aware, there are numerous obstacles to financial independence in our imperfect society.

More people in affluent nations have access to possibilities like inherited money and education that may result in increased financial independence. Compared to those in the Global South, whose economy might be smaller and less stable, individuals in the Global North often have it easier. Although the circumstances are complex, it's important to remember that many individuals are financially disadvantaged for no fault of their own. Your location affects your opportunities for employment, education, and cost of living even inside a country. For instance, career prospects in metropolitan locations are usually better paid than in rural ones, but living in an urban area generally comes with a larger price tag.

Your socioeconomic standing might affect your journey to financial independence regardless of where you reside. Anyone who starts their adult life with some parental guidance and a solid education is more likely to attain their goal of financial independence than someone who does not have these advantages. Additionally, inequality remains a significant obstacle despite certain encouraging advancements. It might be more difficult to attain financial independence if you're a woman, a black person, or you have a disability—all the more reason for us to fight for more fair equality. The world economy may be severely impacted by a variety of factors, including supply-chain problems, geopolitical wars, stock market collapses, and inflation. In the worst cases, these types of worldwide upheavals may result in very serious difficulties for specific individuals, such as lost value for pension funds, property market collapses, and job losses, among many other things.

It would be simple to become bogged down in pessimism, but genuine freedom requires understanding your goals and the obstacles you must overcome. In this manner, you'll be more capable of making wise choices for your particular set of circumstances.

Essential Steps for Reaching Financial Independence

It's obvious from everything we've covered thus far that there are many distinct methods to experience financial independence, and no two strategies are the same. Having said that, there are a few things to remember to steer clear of some typical financial pitfalls and discover a more independent way to handle your finances.

Here is a list of considerations for financial independence, regardless of your desired level of it:

- **Specify your goals**. Determine your ideal life and the potential financial outlay required to realise it, both now and in the future.

- **Pay off any debt with a high-interest rate as soon as you can**. Debt ruins a party, particularly high-interest credit card debt that costs you a fortune. Try to pay off any debt, whether it be this or another sort, as soon as you can to clear your mind and your financial account.
- **Keep aside for dire situations**. It's better to be ready with at least three months' worth of living costs saved up since life occurs. Do your best to put money away in case of unexpected expenses such as home repairs, medical problems, or a broken-down automobile. These may be quite costly.
- **Make a retirement fund contribution**. Whether your goal is to work indefinitely or to take a global tour as soon as you turn sixty, retirement planning is a crucial component of safeguarding your financial future. To increase your savings, make use of

employer-sponsored retirement plans or establish a personal investing portfolio.

- **Buy a house of your own**. Buying your own home or flat might be a fantastic way to accumulate money, but it might not be a choice for everyone. As you become older, you'll be able to save money on housing and leave something for your kids.
- **When you can, invest what you can**. Making passive income is one way to achieve financial success. This might be money amassed in investment accounts or profits from rental properties you own. Despite its associated hazards, investing has the potential to be a very profitable endeavour.

Chapter 3: Building a Strong Financial Foundation: Budgeting, Debt Management, and Savings

Creating a strong financial foundation is essential before starting the wealth development path. Three main pillars support this foundation: savings, debt management, and budgeting. Every pillar is essential to guaranteeing your financial security and setting you up for future expansion.

Taking Charge of Your Finances with Budgeting

Essentially, knowing your income and spending is the foundation of creating a budget. It entails making a strategy to guarantee that your revenue surpasses your expenses, enabling you to invest and save for the future. To get a clear picture of where your money is going, the first step is to keep track of your income and spending for a whole month. Next, divide your spending into three categories: necessities, desires, and savings objectives.

There are several different budgeting techniques available, including the envelope system, the zero-based budget, and the 50/30/20 rule. Try out many approaches to see which one best fits your interests and spending patterns. Whichever approach you use, consistency is essential. As your income or spending fluctuates, examine and revise your budget regularly.

Debt Management: Reducing the Amount Due

Having too much debt may be a major obstacle to building wealth. Excessive interest rates prevent you from saving and investing by trapping you in a loop of payments. As a result, paying off debt ought to come first.

Prioritise paying off your high-interest loans first by identifying them. If you want to cut interest rates and simplify payments, have a look at debt consolidation possibilities. Use techniques such as the debt snowball or avalanche approach to quicken the payback of your debts.

Recall that managing debt does not include paying off all of your debt. Well-managed debt may be deliberately used to increase wealth. Examples of this include mortgages and student loans for expensive degrees. The secret is to properly manage your debt by making sure that your monthly payments don't get in the way of your capacity to invest and save money.

Savings: Creating a Safety Net for Your Money

The foundation of generating wealth is saving. It enables you to save money for investments, unforeseen costs, and long-term objectives. Set aside at least 10% of your monthly salary for savings, and preferably increase that amount as your finances become better.

Numerous saving vehicles are accessible, each with pros and cons of its own. Think about emergency savings, high-yield savings accounts, and retirement accounts such as 401(k)s and IRAs. Every one of them has a distinct function and adds to your overall financial stability.

To maintain consistency and resist the need to squander your funds, automate your savings procedure. You may *"pay yourself first"* and give your financial objectives priority by setting up automatic transfers from your checking account to your savings account.

It takes commitment, preparation, and discipline to lay a solid financial foundation. Establishing a solid savings habit, controlling your debt, and budgeting are the first steps towards a safe and productive financial future.

Recall that being wealthy financially involves more than just acquiring possessions. Achieving financial stability, mental tranquillity, and the liberty to follow your aspirations are the main goals. You give yourself the ability to take charge of your financial future and create the road to abundant and fulfilling life by building a strong financial foundation.

Chapter 4: Developing a Wealth Mindset: Shifting Your Perspective on Money and Abundance

You may have developed a scarcity mentality when it comes to money if you find yourself living "*paycheck to paycheck.*" You may have gone through an incident in the past that has shaped the way you think about money now. You now function from that mental place as a consequence, which gives you less-than-ideal outcomes.

You can discover that you are reluctant to spend money or that you spend the majority of it as soon as it enters your checking account. Although there are undoubtedly emotional aspects to this, your perspective on how you earn and spend money is the most crucial factor of all.

You will always be focused on the idea that you will never have enough if you have a scarcity mentality.

So how can we make the transition from lack to plenty?

Let's start by talking about what constitutes an abundant attitude. An abundant attitude is exactly the reverse of a scarcity mindset, as you may have predicted. When you have an abundant mentality, you may be open to all potential positive outcomes for your financial condition while also keeping them in mind.

Establishing a new company assures you that you will have more than enough clients to meet your financial goals. You don't have the dread of spending money or worrying that you won't have enough of it since you can't do either of those things.

This is due to the abundance mindset's claim that you will always have more money than you need to achieve your goals, regardless of your financial endeavours. Your financial life will follow your energy once you begin to live with this perspective. Your goal of earning and possessing an abundance of money will lead to that.

But if all you think about is scarcity and lack, then it will be all you know about money.

Let's look at some strategies you may use to begin changing your perspective from one of scarcity to one of plenty.

Money Requires Guidance

This is sometimes referred to as having a financial plan or budget. Practically speaking, this makes perfect sense. You won't be able to significantly improve your financial status if you don't have a strategy for your finances. The framework of this plan, however, is based on the idea that to reach your financial objectives, your money requires guidance and a strategy.

Reduce Your Emotional Outlays

Since our emotions are often influenced by the events in our lives, emotional spending is a major problem for a lot of individuals. When things in life don't go as planned, we may feel helpless in the face of turmoil and resort to financial assistance to get things back on track. When life throws you a few curveballs, it's understandable that people turn to money, which symbolises power, to help them feel less pain and more in control.

Money is Not Relative; It Is Personal
Comparing your financial status to that of your friends, relatives, or colleagues is a simple task. This may make you feel inadequate, envious, or hopeless about your financial situation. Think about your financial objectives, not how you think they ought to be related to what you see in other people.

When you see someone driving the newest automobile, you could become envious, but you might not realise that person is struggling to make ends meet each month. However, when you contrast your circumstances, your perspective changes from one of gratitude for what you have to one of insecurity about what you lack.

To prevent a bad change that will unavoidably impact your financial status, it is important to keep money private.

Change the Script for Your Money

Ever find yourself thinking, *I'll never be able to afford that*!" If hold onto the belief that you will never achieve the level of achievement of your affluent pals, then you have come upon a negative money script. Our mental tapestry around money is shaped by money scripts.

They're called money blocks most of the time. Your financial condition may be severely impacted by negative money scripts because your thoughts influence your emotions, which in turn influence the behaviours you perform and, ultimately, the outcomes you achieve. You can see why it's critical to recognise any unfavourable money scripts and replace them with ones that can ultimately mould your financial situation to your advantage.

To begin recognising and changing your scarcity attitude to an abundance mindset, there are many excellent resources to help you. Start-up is surprisingly easy, yet the outcomes are transformative. Bilateral stimulation helps to remove any mental obstacles we could have with money.

Even as you earnestly prepare for your financial future, start by looking at your mentality to discover how you could be undermining yourself as you explore making adjustments to your money.

10 Ways to Change Your Attitude Towards Wealth

You must have a wealth-oriented attitude if you want to draw in and pursue financial achievement.

Everybody has a mentality when it comes to money and wealth; this is the perspective you adopt when you make financial choices. It is critical to have a sound and optimistic wealth attitude if you are to reach your financial and personal objectives. However, it isn't always easy, particularly considering how unpredictable life can be at times and how much forethought is needed to accumulate money.

Moreover, having a good financial attitude takes time to develop. It requires the capacity to remain fully dedicated to reaching your objectives, a strong sense of discipline, the ability to cope with uncertainty with grace, and the ability to maintain an open and adaptable style of thinking throughout time.

These ten insightful suggestions can assist you in changing your perspective and getting started on the path to financial success:

Have Faith in Your Ability

Thinking about achieving financial success is the first step towards achieving it. You will be able to handle your money more wisely if you are resolute in your choice to go on a wealth-building path. You may practise cultivating a positive mentality by telling yourself regularly that you want to succeed financially. You'll feel more secure in enhancing your funds as a result of this.

Decide What You Are Worth

Many people use their financial needs as an excuse to pursue financial gain. To sustain a family is one incentive for some individuals while acquiring assets like a home, vehicle, or other tangible possessions is another. Whatever your reason for wanting to manage your finances, write a list of your goals. This will assist you in identifying the lifestyle you want to lead and in developing a mentality that will enable you to reach your financial goals.

Pay No Attention To What Is Wrong

The worry and anxiety that come with accumulating money is one of the main reasons why most people avoid doing it.

People often shy away from taking financial risks, such as investing or purchasing stocks that might enhance exposure to growth prospects, since money is difficult to grasp and terrible to lose. Reframe your thoughts to be more optimistic and stop concentrating on negatives, such as the amount of debt you have or the obstacles in your path. Don't use derogatory language. Consult with experts outside of your normal social group who have already attained the accomplishment you are aiming for.

Disregard the Past

Everybody has a financial history; some are wealthy from birth, while others have a difficult time getting by. Nonetheless, it's important to put the past behind us and concentrate on the present and future to have a good wealth attitude. Consider what you are doing differently now to secure the lifestyle you want financially. Instead of getting caught up in what you have, concentrate on the riches you are eager to generate.

Appreciate What You Have

A sense of satisfaction is reinforced by affirmations and gratitude. Being grateful for the riches you have so far created is one way to cultivate a positive wealth attitude. Another way is to consistently be aware of what you have. You must affirm that you can increase your money even more and that you are grateful for what you already have if you are to succeed financially.

Make a Vision Board

People often underestimate visualization's effectiveness. Did you know that the majority of financially successful individuals utilise imagery as a technique to cultivate optimism?

Sharing your financial aspirations and objectives via pictures is a terrific way to get started with a vision board. For instance, affix a photo of your ideal house on the board if you want to purchase one. Your vision board will serve as a continual, visible reminder and source of motivation for you to live the life you see and even beyond as you get closer to your objectives.

Prioritise Your Goals

People are better able to ascertain their financial preferences when they set priorities and concentrate on certain objectives. For instance, you'll be in a better mental place to save money if your top goal is to expand your assets.

However, if your top priority is to spend a certain amount of money on experiences and travel, you will be able to make financial concessions in other areas and save or increase your wealth to reach your objectives.

Continue Learning

A person's financial thinking is significantly influenced by their level of financial knowledge and expertise. To increase your confidence in your financial knowledge, enrol in a course or schedule a consultation with a financial adviser to obtain the answers to your queries regarding money management. Your financial judgements will be better informed the more money management you know.

Pardon Your Errors

It might be detrimental to your wealth attitude to feel bad about financial errors. If you forget to pay a bill or credit card payment on time, it's not the end of the world, but it's not acceptable to feel bad about it or put yourself through guilt. Recognise your financial errors and concentrate on making progress. Motivate yourself to feel good rather than guilty so that you won't make the same errors again.

Strive for Positive Self-Progression

Any financially successful individual will tell you that you have to constantly push yourself if you want to reach your financial goals. Pushing oneself entails moving beyond your comfort zone, taking chances, and giving up something to achieve your goals. Encourage and urge yourself every day to do better if you want to improve your financial circumstances.

If you are determined to make a big difference in your financial status, start by making changes to your mindset, spending patterns, and financial literacy.

PART 2:
STRATEGIES FOR
WEALTH CREATION

Chapter 5: Investing for Growth: Exploring Different Investment Vehicles and Strategies

Although financial preferences and methods vary widely, the most basic goal of investing is usually to increase your money's value. The optimal strategy to achieve this objective will differ depending on the investor's time horizon and risk tolerance, among other things. Nonetheless, there are a few fundamental ideas and methods that work for a wide range of development plans and investor kinds.

What is Growth Investing?

While any kind of return on capital, like income on a bond or certificate of deposit (CD), may help you grow your money, the goal of growth investing is to increase your wealth via either short- or long-term capital appreciation. The *offensive* part of an investment portfolio is usually seen as growth investing, while the "defensive" component is devoted to capital preservation, income production, and tax reduction.

In the context of stocks, "*growth*" refers to a company's significant potential for capital expansion, as opposed to value investing, which is the belief held by analysts that a company's stock is undervalued for reasons that are anticipated to alter in the near future. All stocks and stock mutual funds are categorised by independent financial research firm Morningstar as either growth, value, or hybrid (growth + value) investments.

Frequently Used Growth Investment Types

Historically, the most growth potential has been shown by a few primary asset types. They all include equity in one way or another, and they are often riskier.

Some examples of growth investment types are as follows:

Small-Cap Securities

A company's market capitalization or net value determines its size. The term "*small-cap*" in relation to micro, mid, and large-cap companies is not precisely defined, however, most analysts define it as any business with a value of between $300 million and $2 billion.

These companies are often still in the early stages of development, and the price of their stocks might rise significantly. While small-cap stocks have traditionally outperformed their blue-chip counterparts in terms of returns, they also come with a greater degree of risk and volatility. Additionally, during times of economic recovery, small-cap stocks have often outperformed large-cap companies.

Stocks in Technology and Healthcare

For investors seeking a high-yield investment for their portfolios, companies that create new technology or provide advancements in healthcare might be great options. Stocks of businesses that create well-liked or ground-breaking goods might see exponential price increases in a short amount of time.

Investing Speculatively

High-risk growth instruments like penny stocks, futures and options contracts, foreign exchange, and speculative real estate like undeveloped land are popular among thrill-seekers and speculators. For high-income, aggressive investors, there are also private equity and partnerships for oil and gas drilling. Making the proper decisions in this area may result in a return on capital that is many times more than the original investment, but it is also possible to lose every last penny of your principal.

Examining Growth Stocks

When assessing investment growth, there are many important aspects to take into account. The amount of money that investors leave depends largely on several factors, including growth rate, kind and quantity of risk, and other aspects of investment.

Among the information that experts and growth investors look at when it comes to stocks is this:

Return On Equity (ROE)

The ability of a company to turn a profit is expressed mathematically as return on equity (ROE). It is expressed as a percentage that is calculated by dividing the net income of the business—in this example, the revenue left over after preferred stockholders have received their dividends but before common stock distributions are paid—by the total equity held by shareholders.

For instance, if two corporations have $100 million in total shareholder equity and $300 million in total shareholder equity, with $75 million in net income for the year, respectively, the company with the smaller shareholder equity is offering a higher return on equity since it is generating the same amount of net income with less equity.

A Rise in EPS, or Earnings Per Share

A firm whose earnings per share are rising over time is most likely doing something correctly, even if there are several forms of EPS and the amount of money made per share does not always provide a complete picture of how a business is operated. Investors often target businesses with rising earnings per share (EPS), but further investigation is necessary to confirm that these figures reflect actual cash flow from legal company operations.

Estimated Revenue

Projected earnings releases are closely watched by many day traders and short-term investors since they may impact a company's stock price both now and in the future. A lot of investors profit by trading earnings releases.

For instance, if a firm reports higher-than-expected results, the stock price will often increase swiftly before declining again in the days that follow. On the other hand, a steady stream of optimistic profit estimates will eventually support a stock increase.

Examining Various Investment Vehicles and Strategies

Investing may be intimidating, particularly if you are unfamiliar with the idea of money management in general. If the latter describes you, read our earlier blog article on the fundamentals of making and adhering to a financial plan. We are dissecting popular investment alternatives, such as stocks, bonds, mutual funds, ETFs, and real estate, to assist you in navigating the world of investing. Knowing these possibilities can help you make well-informed investing decisions that fit your risk tolerance.

Mutual Funds: The Best Experience for Carpooling

A mutual fund functions similarly to carpooling in that a qualified fund manager drives the vehicle, collecting money from several participants and using it to build a diverse portfolio of stocks, bonds, and other assets. Diversification is mutual funds' primary benefit. Mutual funds expose investors to a variety of sectors and industries while lowering the risk associated with individual investments by owning a variety of assets. Furthermore, modest investors may engage in the financial markets with very little cash because of mutual funds' accessibility.

Invest in Stocks to Quicken Your Wealth

Stocks, which stand for ownership in a firm, are sometimes referred to as shares or equity. Equities may provide thrilling profits, but they can have ups and downs, much like the rush of operating a fast automobile. Purchasing stock in a firm enables you to become a shareholder and a percentage of the company's equity. You may get dividends, which are the company's earnings given to shareholders, and you are entitled to a part of the profits as a shareholder. Regarding the twists that may occur, be aware that the performance of the firm and the state of the market might cause your stocks' value to increase or decrease.

Examine a company's financial health, industry performance, and management stability carefully before investing in its stock. Better still, keep an eye out for our weekly stock recommendations.

Bonds: Consistent and Dependable Operators

Governments and other organisations issue bonds as financial instruments or debt securities to raise money. Travelling at the steady pace of fixed income, this trustworthy car provides a secure and steady ride. Investing in bonds is effectively lending money to the issuer for a certain amount of time, in exchange for periodical interest payments from the issuer. The issuer repays the bondholder the principal amount on the bond's maturity date. Keep in mind that bonds usually provide smaller returns than equities. Although bonds may not provide investors with the same sense of excitement as stocks, they do offer a steady path for those looking for a more dependable path.

ETFs (Exchange-Traded Funds): A Traditional Transformer Investment

Exchange-traded funds (ETFs) are flexible investment vehicles that provide you the ability to personalise your journey by combining the finest aspects of individual equities and mutual funds. ETFs contain a variety of underlying assets, including stocks, bonds, and commodities, much as mutual funds do. ETFs, on the other hand, trade on stock markets just like individual equities, unlike mutual funds. ETFs are designed to follow the performance of a certain asset class, index, industry, or commodity. Because of the trading flexibility of ETFs, investors may purchase and sell shares at market prices at any time throughout the trading day. ETFs are different from mutual funds in that they have this functionality instead of being valued after each trading day.

Real Estate: Travelling on Concrete Ground

Buying, holding, and managing real estate to earn income and capital growth makes real estate an appealing investment option. It's similar to travelling a beautiful path across land, where every mile represents a possible source of revenue. Investments in real estate may take many different forms, ranging from commercial assets like office buildings, retail stores, and industrial facilities to residential properties like homes and apartments. It offers the chance for property values to increase over time. It provides the chance to earn consistent rental revenue. Leveraging via home finance is possible, which might increase yields.

Lastly, since real estate investments often have a low connection with conventional financial assets like stocks and bonds, they provide advantages for diversification. This may assist in lowering an investment portfolio's total risk.

Making decisions in the complex world of investing may be made easier by being aware of the many possibilities accessible. Although stocks have more risks, they also have the potential for large profits. Bonds provide consistent income and stability, but they have smaller yields. Real estate investments provide physical assets with the potential for income and gain, while mutual funds and exchange-traded funds (ETFs) give accessibility to the financial markets and diversity.

Building a well-balanced investing plan might be aided by diversifying your portfolio across different investment possibilities. Keep in mind that there are dangers associated with any investments, and consulting a financial advisor may help you create an appropriate strategy that fits your specific situation.

The Final Word

Growth investment is a complicated topic that is often studied in conjunction with other topics including market research, technical analysis, and fundamental analysis. Both individual and institutional investors use a plethora of other development tactics, many of which would be far outside the purview of this paper. See your broker or financial adviser for further details on investment growth options.

Chapter 6: Generating Passive Income: Creating Multiple Streams of Revenue

Do you want to establish many revenue streams and diversify your sources of income? You're in luck if so.

This section of the book will look at 12 tried-and-true strategies for creating numerous revenue sources. You may experiment with a range of revenue sources, from just adding active and passive income streams to side gigs and more.

Along with talking about the value of diversifying your sources of income, I'll also provide some practical advice on how to get started.

Now let's get going.

Invest in Property

One of the most well-liked strategies for creating many passive income investment streams is real estate.

You may profit from capital gains, rental income, and other passive income streams by investing in real estate.

Moreover, real estate is a physical asset, which facilitates the diversification of your sources of passive income.

You may become a landlord by making an initial purchase of an already-existing property.

In addition to the possible reward from capital gains when you ultimately decide to sell, this will allow you to get rental income.

As an alternative, you may invest in a vacation rental or a home in the Airbnb style and earn rental revenue from visitors to your neighbourhood.

Investing in real estate via a REIT (real estate investment trust) is an additional option.

With a REIT, you may combine your funds with those of other investors to benefit from their combined purchasing power.

You may invest in a portfolio of properties via a REIT and take advantage of the dividends that are distributed to shareholders.

You may generate a consistent income stream and profit from the gradual increase in property prices by making real estate investments.

But it's crucial to remember that real estate investment has risks, so make sure you do your homework before committing.

Think About Launching a Company

Creating a company might be a fantastic way to have many sources of income. Owning your own company gives you access to a variety of revenue streams, including internet revenue streams.

You may easily develop seven streams of income, such as selling goods and services and making money from advertising, depending on your kind of company.

You must first develop a solid company concept and figure out how to make money off of it. This might include developing an app, selling handcrafted goods, or providing advisory services.

After selecting a company strategy, you should ascertain the most effective means of bringing in money. This might be creating an online shop, finding affiliates to market your goods or services, or running advertisements for your offerings.

Additionally, you'll need to plan how to get funds for your company and do research. To get your firm off the ground, you may need to take out a loan or use crowdsourcing.

You should also have a strategy in place for advertising and marketing your company.

You may utilise this to draw in more clients if you produce films or other material about your company.

All things considered, launching a company is a terrific method to generate various revenue sources.

You may easily have many sources of income and generate money from various streams provided you put in the necessary effort and attention.

Establish a Source of Passive Income

One of the greatest methods to generate several revenue streams is to establish a passive income stream. You may earn a consistent, dependable stream of income from this kind of work that can support your main source of income or be used as a second source without having to exchange your time for money.

A variety of strategies exist for generating passive income streams, such as investing in stocks, bonds, real estate, and other financial instruments; starting an internet company; leasing out real estate; and taking part in affiliate marketing schemes.

It's important to thoroughly consider what kind of passive income will be most beneficial for you before starting to build passive income streams.

Peer-to-peer lending, dividend stock investments, real estate investments, and affiliate marketing are a few of the top passive income options.

You may utilise the rental income from your real estate investment to augment your main source of income.

By receiving monthly dividends from the companies you own, dividend investing may also assist you in creating a passive income stream.

While engaging in affiliate marketing programmes might earn you fees from purchases you make, peer-to-peer lending can provide you with a consistent flow of revenue from loans you make and repayments you get.

Creating a passive income stream may be a terrific approach to creating extra streams of money, regardless of the passive income strategy you decide on.

It's critical to do due diligence and determine which kind of passive income plan will be most beneficial to you.

You may generate a consistent secondary income stream with the correct approach and commitment, giving you additional cash for savings or personal usage.

Write and Sell Electronic Books

One of the easiest strategies to create many passive income streams is to write an eBook. It requires little effort and may be completed at any moment.

Selling eBooks is a fantastic method to generate passive income as they can be found on a variety of websites, such as Amazon.

Simply composing the material and submitting it is all that is required. You'll have a reliable stream of revenue when the eBook is launched. Although writing an eBook requires time and work, the benefits are priceless.

Any topic you're enthusiastic about may be the subject of your writing, and there are many methods to make money from it. For instance, you may build a membership website where users must pay to view your material or use affiliate links.

It's a fantastic method to begin generating passive money and diversify your sources of revenue.

Create T-Shirts

Creating t-shirt designs is an excellent method to have many sources of income.

You may not only make designs that fit your aesthetic, but you can also market such designs to those who value them. It's simple to post your designs to online stores so that others may buy them.

You may even sell your designs in person or on Etsy by printing them out.

It's a fantastic method to monetize something you already like doing, and it has the potential to develop into a steady source of revenue.

You may provide custom t-shirt printing services in addition to coming up with original designs.

Many businesses are prepared to pay for their shirts to be designed and printed by a third party. If you decide to put some work into it, this might become a terrific side job or possibly your main source of money.

You may also collaborate with nearby companies and groups to provide embroidery and mass printing for merchandising items like coats, caps, and sweatshirts.

Creating t-shirt designs is an excellent method to expand your sources of revenue.

Selling your designs will earn you money, or you may provide bespoke printing services. In any case, you will undoubtedly earn some money doing what you love.
Why not attempt it then?

Market Handmade Items
One of the most well-liked options for numerous sources of income is making and selling handmade things.
Making crafts such as jewellery, cards, knitted products, and decorations may be a profitable and enjoyable way to make money. To display your work and sell your goods, it's simple to launch a website or blog or to open an online shop or marketplace like Etsy or eBay.
You can locate local craft fairs and events on several sites, which you may use to market and sell your goods.
Selling your crafts may earn you money if you have a good marketing plan in place and can quickly grow your client base.

Provide Independent Contractor Services

Offering freelance services may be a fantastic strategy to diversify your revenue streams and create another source of income. You may provide a variety of services, including writing, content production, SEO optimisation, graphic design, web building, and more. You have the option of working directly with companies or via internet marketplaces like Fiverr and Upwork.

Offering freelancing services as one of your revenue streams has many benefits. It enables you to work remotely, which eliminates the need for you to travel or be at a certain location to do your job.
Additionally, you have the freedom to choose the kind of project you want to work on, which enables you to focus on a certain

skill you have and earn more money doing it.

And last, working as a freelancer may help you save more money and have a steady stream of income.
It's important to establish a strong online presence and portfolio if you want to make freelancing your primary source of income. In addition to having accounts on various freelance networks, make sure you have a website or portfolio displaying your work.
Make a list of your services and talents as well, so prospective customers will know what you can do for them.

Finally, to improve your chances of landing a job, promote yourself and let others know about your offerings. Freelancing may be a terrific way to diversify your sources of income and create an additional revenue stream provided you put in the necessary planning and develop a solid marketing plan.

Rent a Room in Your House

One simple approach to creating a second source of income is to rent out a room in your home. It's a fantastic approach to add additional cash from another source to your primary source of income.

Renting out a room in your house might be a terrific way to start, whether you need money for short-term costs or long-term solutions.

You may choose to rent out all of the space or just a portion of it when renting out a room. If you have a spare bedroom, for instance, you could rent the whole space to a single renter or split it up into two areas and rent out each one individually.

To avoid misunderstanding or confrontation, make sure you and the renter have clear limits in both situations. Additionally, you may choose whether to lease your accommodation for a certain amount of time or an extended period.

Although short-term rentals are often more lucrative, they also take more work since you have to consistently locate new renters.

However, since you will only need to locate new renters occasionally, long-term leases take less work.

Do your homework on local rental property rules and regulations before renting out your space.

When renting out a room, there may be certain guidelines and regulations that you need to go by in some locations.

To safeguard yourself in the event of accidents or damage sustained while your renters are residing in your house, you should also think about getting landlord insurance.

Finally, as an additional source of income, renting out a room in your house is a great method to augment your current income with a money market fund.

You may simply maximise the possibilities of this revenue stream and benefit from additional money with proper preparation and study.

Purchase Dividend Stocks

Purchasing dividend-paying stocks is a great method to create an additional revenue stream.

Publicly listed corporations that routinely provide dividends to their shareholders are considered dividend stocks.

Investing in dividend stocks is a terrific strategy to diversify your income sources and establish a steady, passive income stream, even if the amount of dividends you get may fluctuate.

It's crucial to research the companies that will provide you with the highest returns and the most reliable dividends when investing in dividend stocks.

Patience is also required when investing in dividend stocks since the gains may not come in right away.

On the other hand, dividend stock investment may be a great method to diversify your income sources and establish a reliable secondary income stream provided you are patient and do your homework.

Engage in Affiliate Marketing Initiatives

Creating several revenue streams and diversifying your sources of income may be achieved via affiliate marketing.

By promoting other people's goods or services, you may use affiliate marketing to make money off of each transaction.

Because affiliate programs usually have very little overhead, you may start making money right away and generating new revenue streams and passive income with little work on your part.

Let's take an example where you sign up for an affiliate program for a service or product you currently use and like.
You may begin advertising the product or service on your website, blog, or social media accounts as soon as you sign up for the program.
You are paid a commission each time a customer uses your link to make a purchase.
With only a few clicks to get started, this is an excellent example of a side source of revenue.

Adding new passive income streams to your portfolio via affiliate marketing is another excellent strategy.
You won't need to make any more effort after you've put up the first link to advertise the product or service and can begin making passive revenue.

For anyone searching for additional passive income ideas that don't demand a lot of additional labour, this is an excellent alternative that requires other sources.

All things considered, affiliate marketing is a fantastic approach to start earning passive money and diversify your sources of revenue.

It is easy to start and doesn't need any specialised knowledge or abilities.

Consider signing up for an affiliate marketing program right now if you're searching for a side job to generate passive income or just want to earn some additional cash.

Online Product Sales

One of the most popular strategies to have many streams of income is to sell items online.

There are a plethora of venues available for businesses to market their products and services, regardless of whether they are antique, handcrafted, or secondhand goods. Selling goods online may lead to a variety of revenue streams, including affiliate commissions, advertising costs, and recurring membership fees.

You may sell a wide variety of goods, including fashion, electronics, and digital goods like ebooks and lessons.

Furthermore, several approaches to product marketing may help you maximise the potential of your revenue streams.

You may market your items and boost sales in a variety of methods, including social media, email marketing campaigns, and PPC advertising.

All things considered, making money online via product sales is a terrific method to supplement current income and establish new revenue sources.

Entrepreneurs may take advantage of this chance to create a lucrative company and many revenue streams with the appropriate platform and marketing plan.

Make a Peer-to-Peer Loan Investment
An alternative to standard savings accounts that has the potential to provide greater returns is peer-to-peer (P2P) lending.
In essence, peer-to-peer lending is borrowing money from investors instead of banks.
For those who want to come up with secondary income ideas and numerous sources of money, this is a terrific alternative. Investors using peer-to-peer lending can pick which borrowers they work with and what interest rates they are ready to pay.

Numerous loan types are available for investment, including personal, student, and corporate loans. The degree of risk involved in peer-to-peer lending is contingent upon the creditworthiness of the borrower.

Investing in peer-to-peer lending is comparatively simple. Choosing a platform that will make the loan procedure easier is a good place to start.

After deciding on a platform, you may look for possible borrowers and make your selections based on the information in their loan applications.

After that, you'll be able to keep an eye on the loan's repayment and modify your investment as necessary.

All things considered, P2P lending is a desirable choice for investors wishing to diversify their holdings and produce cash flow from many sources of primary and secondary income ideas. It may help you diversify your portfolio, assist others by giving finance to individuals in need, and provide great returns with an upfront investment.

Chapter 7: Building Your Career: Strategies for Earning More and Achieving Financial Goals

Why delay thinking about how to achieve your financial objectives if you haven't begun already? You may plan for the future and get a high degree of enjoyment by putting wise financial ideas into practice.

I have included financial techniques in this book to assist you in reaching your financial objectives.

1. Put Your Objectives in Writing and Then See Them

Without a strategy, achieving anything is difficult. Start by outlining your financial goals, a timeline for reaching your aim, a method for measuring progress, and the actions you'll take to guarantee it. After you've written everything down, picture it.

You may accomplish any goal, even financial goals, with the aid of visualisation, which is a very effective technique. Make your financial plans a mental reality before putting them into action. By doing this, you'll encourage yourself to remain on course and strengthen your confidence in your ability to reach your goals.

2. Examine Your Present Finances and Expenses

Without understanding where you've come from, it will be impossible to follow where you are heading. As a result, you should take some time to consider your present financial status, your frequent spending habits, and any areas where you may cut down on your spending.

You may save the most money by paying particular attention to your spending patterns. This does not imply that you have to start living a modest lifestyle, but you may be able to make a few little monthly savings that you can put back into your financial security.

3. Create an Emergency Fund

An emergency fund and a "freedom" fund are similar. You will have a 6–12 month emergency fund to handle whatever challenges life throws at you, whether they are related to your family, a health issue, or you just wish to take some time off.

To avoid getting off course in the event of an unforeseen circumstance, you must account for both your long-term financial objectives and some flexible emergency funds that you may withdraw immediately. Examine the many investing alternatives available, or just start a savings account. Whichever path you choose, setting aside half of your monthly income for discretionary spending until you have a little emergency fund is a smart place to start when it comes to long-term financial success.

4. Use Free Funds

Your workplace likely provides financial-led benefits like retirement programmes and group life insurance. Although you definitely won't be able to reach your financial objectives with only them, they may still be helpful in the process. However, you must first identify them.

Make sure you familiarise yourself with any perks you get as an employee and read the finer points to understand what they include. Take into consideration features such as health savings accounts and matching contributions. They could serve as a means of accelerating savings accumulation.

5. Adopt a Wealth Acquisition Mentality

You may start now and work towards your financial objectives by increasing your wealth. One advantage of permanent life insurance is that it has a cash-value component, which lets you accumulate money even after you pass away. Many individuals are unaware that life insurance policies exist that are intended to support you and your family members through life and death.

You contribute to both the cash value and death benefit pots when you have permanent insurance. Because the monetary worth of each of these increases with time, you may benefit from having access to cash in your later years. You also have the added advantage of leaving your family a death benefit. That benefits both parties.

6. Consider the Tax

The majority of savings accounts impose taxes on the money you accumulate. However, whatever money you accumulate with a permanent life insurance policy is fully tax-free. This implies that while you enjoy the money you've accumulated, you won't have to worry about sending the IRS a check.

When it comes to accessing your money, a permanent life insurance policy is effectively a tax-free loan against you with no interest because you are unable to pay yourself taxes. The borrowed sum is then paid back by your death benefit upon your passing, with the remaining amount going to your dependents.

7. Increase Portfolio Diversification

By making investments in a variety of account kinds, you may diversify your portfolio. By doing this, you'll have more choices and could even be able to reach your financial objectives more quickly. A wise financial plan also assists you in controlling the risk and maintaining focus on your objectives.

Let's examine savings accounts as an example. To increase your possibilities, why not store your money in many accounts?

There are several methods to save for your future that can enable you to meet your financial objectives a little bit sooner, from stocks and bonds to tax-advantaged life insurance and your 401(K).

8. Consider Starting a Side Business

We're not advocating that you take on excessive duty or burn the candle at both ends. However, starting a side business might be a terrific way to boost your income so you can make wise investment decisions.

There are side gigs that might help you increase your income flow, even if adding 20 hours a week to your full-time employment might not be the greatest use of your time. For instance, is there anything you can do to supplement your income from your day job with a hobby?

9. Seek Expert Guidance

There are several places online where you may get financial advice in addition to reading this book. Seeing things from a different angle might help you concentrate on things you weren't previously thinking about and expand your mind to new concepts.

You might consult with a financial expert, who will evaluate your existing financial situation and assist you in establishing reasonable objectives. They are often expensive, but sometimes you have to make a little short-term investment to reap the long-term benefits.

10. Make Arrangements to Prepare for Your Retirement

Retirement may not be fully included in your financial plans since you are mostly considering the medium- and short-term scenarios. However, anybody hoping to live a financially independent life should consider how they will pay for their later years.

To make sure your objectives are on track to support you in later life, check your retirement savings strategy. This might include making use of the 401(K) plan offered by your work, assessing your present spending patterns and budget, and obtaining a life insurance policy that will take care of you in old age, which gets us neatly to our bonus round.

Bonus: Obtain a Policy of Permanent Life Insurance

Let's get straight to the point: getting a permanent life insurance policy is a terrific method to reach your financial objectives. Its tax-free savings and cash-value feature allow you to accumulate wealth over time. What could be wrong with that?

Additionally, your rates are fixed from the moment you enrol and won't go up as long as you keep the policy. As a result, it's a wise investment to make in your 20s and 30s and may complement other financial methods to help you achieve your financial goals.

It also includes a death benefit, so in the worst-case scenario, you might ensure that your loved ones won't face financial hardship after your passing. Consider permanent life insurance as a comprehensive plan to help you cover all the bases.

In summary: identifying the most effective financial tactics Using these pointers, you may boost your self-assurance in your financial situation. You will be able to create wealth, achieve your financial objectives, and look forward to the future if you have the correct vision, work hard, and figure out the best strategy to invest.

Chapter 8:
Entrepreneurship: Launching Your Business and Achieving Financial Independence

The goal of any entrepreneur is to operate a lucrative and successful company. More significantly, the goal of any entrepreneur is to become financially independent at some time in their life. Being an entrepreneur is a great way to become financially independent, but it's a long and challenging journey.

How To Become Financially Independent Through Your Own Business

It is possible to guarantee the market success of your company if you have the necessary abilities and mentality. After that, you'll be able to enjoy the fruits of both your initial efforts and your hard work. The issue is that company ownership is seldom as simple as the owners first think. It is impossible to foresee exactly what will occur or how things will work out. But you can make sure you don't make expensive blunders by planning. Having said that, here are a few strategies for using business to achieve financial independence.

Make a Plan First
Take a step back and decide what it is you want to accomplish with your life before you go farther into the realm of business. Stated differently, what does one mean by financial independence? Many company owners define financial independence as being able

to enjoy earnings worry-free and with no debt.

You have to put money first if you want your firm to be debt-free. You won't become financially or otherwise independent by overspending. As a result, make a strategy for how you're going to accomplish your objectives and devise methods for saving money rather than spending it all at once. Your firm's revenues may entice you to start spending immediately and having fun, but you have to understand that managing a business involves more than just making money.

Recognise Your Financial Situation

A common misconception among company owners is that their revenue is a reflection of their riches. Regretfully, your wealth does not equal your salary. You may become financially independent more quickly with a high-earning company, but the secret is to continue saving more money than you make. Thus, you should put in the effort to comprehend your financial situation.

Revenue may be generated from commercial revenues, but there are always expenditures associated with running a business, including overhead and other charges. Upon computing your business's assets and liabilities, you will ultimately determine your earnings or capital gains. You will ultimately accumulate enough savings to make significant investments and optimise your earnings if you maintain minimum consumption, that is if you refrain from immediately spending gains.

Stay Away from Debt
It's much easier said than done while operating a company to avoid debt. Your debt is a reflection of your company's financial health. A low personal credit score,

for example, might result in a bank loan being denied or in very high-interest rates and unfavourable payback terms. Make sure you take care of your funds before beginning your endeavour.

One effective method of managing your obligations and paying them off is via debt consolidation. Consolidating debt is taking out a bigger loan with more acceptable terms and circumstances to pay off other outstanding obligations. In this manner, you may concentrate on just one debt rather than many smaller ones, avoiding missed or late payments as well as additional costs. Achieving financial independence and operating a profitable company rely on effective money management and debt avoidance.

Employ Your Profits Sensibly

As previously said, you can feel pressured to spend your money rather than put it aside for chances down the road. It is best not to do that. Rather, consider how you might prudently use your earnings. Earnings have the potential to compound, but only if you use them wisely. For instance, major investments need financial resources.

You have to make sure that your company always has positive cash flow to do that. Additionally, make sure that any gains you save are maintained apart from other accounts in an emergency savings account. Don't forget to add investments to your retirement savings. Take 401(k) plans and individual retirement accounts (IRAs or Roth IRAs) as examples. Every strategy offers different tax benefits that might enable you to set aside money to achieve financial independence.

One of the most effective paths to financial freedom can be entrepreneurship. But becoming an entrepreneur also means taking calculated risks. Numerous entrepreneurs fail in their ventures, demonstrating that managing a firm involves more than just turning a profit. You won't be able to enjoy the results of your hard work if you're not ready to assume the responsibilities of operating a firm.

PART 3:
MAINTAINING AND GROWING YOUR WEALTH

Chapter 9: Protecting Your Assets: Insurance, Risk Management, and Estate Planning

One important but sometimes ignored part of financial planning is asset protection. Two essential elements that may protect your money, provide your loved ones financial stability, and guarantee that your assets are dispersed in accordance with your preferences are estate planning and insurance. We will discuss the value of estate planning and insurance in this blog article and the reasons they need to be a crucial component of your overall financial plan.

Insurance: Shielding Yourself and Your Loved Ones

- *Life insurance*: In the case of your death, life insurance offers your loved ones a financial safety net. It may guarantee your family's financial security by paying for last costs, unpaid bills, and missed wages.
- *Health insurance:* Health insurance gives you access to high-quality healthcare services and shields you from the exorbitant expenses of medical treatment. Preventive care, prescription drug costs, hospital stays, and doctor visits are all covered.
- *Property insurance*: It protects your priceless possessions, such as your house and furnishings, from unforeseen calamities like fires, thefts, and natural catastrophes.

Estate Planning: Securing Your Legacy

- *Will*: By writing a will, you may direct the distribution of your possessions after your passing. It minimises the possibility of disagreements among family members and guarantees that your desires are followed.
- *Trust*: A trust offers a more thorough and adaptable method of allocating assets. It may lessen estate taxes, aid in preventing probate, and safeguard assets for future generations.
- *Power of attorney*: If you are incapacitated, a power of attorney designates someone you trust to handle financial and legal decisions on your behalf.

The Advantages of Estate Planning and Insurance

1. *Financial security*: Insurance offers financial security and peace of mind by acting as a safety net against unforeseen circumstances.

2. *Asset protection*: By ensuring that your assets are dispersed in accordance with your preferences, estate planning helps to minimise possible conflicts and safeguard your legacy.

3. *Tax efficiency*: Making the most of the transfer of wealth to your beneficiaries and minimising estate taxes are two benefits of estate planning.

4. *Family protection*: To safeguard your family ones' financial security and general well-being, insurance and estate planning are essential.

Seeking Expert Advice

Because insurance and estate planning may be complicated, it's a good idea to see an expert to help you evaluate your requirements, get the right coverage, and draft an extensive estate plan that is customised to your unique situation.

Planning for Asset Protection and Risk Management

Every investor needs to consider the risks associated with assisted living, catastrophic disease or disability, property loss, and professional, company, and personal responsibility. Protecting your financial health is one of our responsibilities, and it could include working with you to reduce your exposure to certain risks. Purchasing health, life, long-term care, and disability insurance, shifting asset ownership, and taking advantage of other legal safeguards are a few examples of risk management strategies.

Planning for Asset Protection

Asset protection planning aims to transfer the risk of these events by acquiring health, life, long-term care, and disability insurance, repositioning asset ownership, and other legal protections. Lawsuits, accidents, property damage, and other financial risks are realities of everyday life. There are risks involved with starting and operating a company.

How protected your personal and corporate assets are against danger depends on several things. Among them are:
- The kind of company structure you choose
- Which state did you decide to do business in and how do you run your company
- Your personnel
- Your income

Your choices for managing these risks are identified via business risk management. We work to make sure you are satisfied with the amount of risk you are accepting, from business protection to your health. While many tasks in the risk management process may be completed by financial experts, others call for the knowledge of insurance specialists. If you want to concentrate on risk management, we could collaborate closely with an insurance expert. Effective risk management is essential to wealth management, and a well-designed insurance plan will work in harmony with your broader business, investment, tax, estate, and retirement strategies.

In Summary

Preserving your money and ensuring financial stability require you to safeguard your assets with insurance and estate planning. It is possible to protect yourself and your loved ones from financial difficulties, preserve your legacy, and guarantee that your assets are transferred in accordance with your preferences by putting suitable insurance policies into place and developing a thoughtful estate plan. Make the required preparations now to safeguard your most valuable assets and provide a strong basis for the future.

Chapter 10: Leaving a Legacy: Philanthropy, Financial Literacy, and Empowering Others

There are many opportunities to broaden your influence and have an effect on the world around you, even beyond the personal satisfaction that comes from reaching your economic objectives and obtaining financial stability. A lasting impact on other people's lives and a constructive contribution to the common good are the ultimate measures of success, which go beyond just financial gain. This chapter examines three effective ways—philanthropy, financial literacy, and empowerment—that you may use your financial knowledge and assets to provide a significant and lasting legacy.

Philanthropy

Giving back to your community or causes that are important to you is more than just being kind. Choosing to use your money to solve social issues, give to deserving organisations, and build a better future is a deliberate choice.

Philanthropy may take many different forms, such as creating your endowment, giving your time and skills as a volunteer, or making direct gifts to foundations and charitable organisations. Whether you're supporting environmental protection, critical medical treatment to neglected populations, or educational projects, your charitable efforts may have a significant effect.

Selecting the appropriate charitable route needs serious thought. You'll feel fulfilled and like you have a purpose if your contributions are in line with your beliefs and interests. Think about issues that speak to you personally or places where you think your contributions may have a big impact. It's important to conduct your homework on possible beneficiaries to make sure your contributions go to respectable organisations with a successful track record. Think about the format of your contributions as well. While endowment funds provide a stable and enduring source of income for future generations, recurring gifts give long-term support.

Financial Literacy

A vital tool for giving people and communities the ability to take charge of their financial futures is financial literacy. You may motivate others to handle their money wisely, make educated financial choices, and reach their financial objectives by imparting your financial knowledge and experience. This may be accomplished in a number of ways, including:

1. Mentorship programmes: Offering personalised advice and assistance to those who want to become more financially literate.
2. Providing educational lectures and workshops on subjects like debt management, investment, and budgeting.
3. Developing websites, blogs, or social media platforms with easily accessible financial education content is one way to provide online resources.
4. assisting current projects: collaborating with well-known financial literacy groups to expand their influence and audience.
5. Giving people the information and ability to handle their money wisely gives them the ability to escape the cycle of debt, provide a safe future for themselves and their children, and

make more significant contributions to the economy.

Empowerment

True riches go beyond having a lot of money. It includes having the capacity to take charge of your life, make wise choices, and meaningfully engage with your community. Giving people the tools they need to accomplish these goals is the basis of a lasting legacy. This may entail:

- Supporting small businesses: Making investments in and providing mentorship to company owners, especially those from underrepresented groups, to promote economic expansion and employment creation.
- Proposing changes to laws: Making arguments for laws that favour equitable opportunity, financial inclusion, and access to education.

- Advancing social justice entails making use of your position and resources to support issues related to social justice and the rights of underrepresented communities.
- Telling your story: motivating others by sharing your personal story of overcoming obstacles and attaining financial success.
- Positive change cascades from you when you use your resources and influence to empower others. You help create a society that is more fair and equal, where everyone has the chance to prosper and realise their full potential.

Conclusion

Leaving a legacy that transcends personal riches is a laudable endeavour, which is possible. Through embracing empowerment, financial knowledge, and generosity, you can make a long-lasting beneficial difference in the world.

Every act of kindness, every information exchange, and every attempt to empower others goes towards creating a brighter future for future generations.

It's important to keep in mind that genuine wealth comes from leaving a legacy as well as from accumulating resources as you travel your path to financial success.